CROSSING
COCYTUS

CROSSING COCYTUS
Poems by Paul Mariani

THE GROVE PRESS POETRY SERIES
EDITED BY ROBERT PACK

GROVE PRESS, INC.,/NEW YORK

First Edition 1982
First Printing 1982
ISBN: 0-394-52829-8
Library of Congress Catalog Card Number: 81-48539

First Evergreen Edition 1982
First Printing 1982
ISBN: 0-394-17978-1
Library of Congress Catalog Card Number: 81-48539

Library of Congress Cataloging in Publication Data

Mariani, Paul L.
    Crossing Cocytus.

    I. Title.
PS3563.A6543C7   811'.54   81-48539
ISBN 0-394-52829-8   AACR2
ISBN 0-394-17978-1 (1st Evergreen ed.)

Manufactured in the United States of America

GROVE PRESS, INC., 196 West Houston Street, New York, N.Y. 10014

THE GROVE PRESS POETRY SERIES edited by Robert Pack

The men too need each other.
This book, then, is for seven
who listened: for Dave and Ed
and Gary the woodsman, and for John and
Mike and Ron and my brother Walter:
my own poor man's philosopher's
circle, philosopher's stone.

Contents

III   *Promptings*

I   *Secrets*

Bondswomen of the royal retinue,
Since you too are participants in this act
Of intercession, give me your advice.
What shall I say to dedicate these gifts,
What words contrive to please my father's ear?
That I have brought them from a loving wife
To her dear lord, an offering from my mother?

Song

*Sing me a song, she said, once
before I die. A song with love
in it . . . and memories.*

A lifetime's thought to do that,
and maybe even then a miss,
I mused, shuffling across
the stage. In the beginning: young
you, not yet sweet sixteen, standing
at the counter while the truckers
swilled down hash and eggs and
coffee, calling softly out to him,
begging he might come round back
a moment so you might tell him
you were pregnant. O had you gone
the way the smart girls went
then there wouldn't be this song.

Sing me a song, she said.

             Two feet
swollen mutton size, swaddled
thick in bandages and sulphur stuff,
big baby in his carriage who'd tried
to take a bath in boiling water.
If the thing don't work, the doctor
said, we can always cut them off
above the ankles.

A head broken
ramming it against an iron post
in a city sidewalk game of hide
and seek, blood all over the seat
of the Yellow Checker cab
as your voice began to crack.

A song about the good times.

Your oldest holding the broken
whiskey bottle still, pulled from
the grocer's garbage can, while
your second baby howled
through the funny gash where his mouth
and teeth had been.
                              In sixteen
years: seven little indians and three
or four more dead. No money
and big dreams. The solace too
of can't you eat them friggen eggs
without drooling on the plate. Croon
croon. O one by one them kiddos left
as fast they could: army, navy,
seminary, school, even hump bump
psychedelic van and California.
Lawrence Welk—a one and a two—
and disappearing acts with fifths
and a shuffle out the door.

Auld lang's syne. A song, a
bloody song. Sing me a song
about all them good times . . .

ha! before the lawyers got
the house, the car, and the whey-
faced turds in grey three-piece
suits grabbed the little business?

All together now:

> *Good, better, best,*
> *Never let it rest . . .*

And beg, borrow, steal, to keep
those beneficial creditors at bay
until, like the fledgling pelicans
that lacerate the mother's breast
to feed, we finally bled you dry.

Sing me a song, a song. A song
to soothe a tired woman. Something
with love in it . . . and memories.

Entrance Song

Begin there: with the watery light
of early winter, steady, brimful, as if
once again refreshed from that secret source,
the book still open to the passage
on the Visitation, the passage of the Woman

to her cousin's, the two rejoicing
as in the old tapestry, both filled with child.
Women: ubiquitous and changing as the air itself,
as in a dream, as in a mirror in a window
fronting the busy thoroughfare, filling

a man at all stages of his life. What might
have been and what is, as in the merging
of two rivers, woman realized and the Perfect
Woman. Source and source. The lake, the heaving
chestnut in the full of summer as she lay there,

arms outstretched and beckoning, steady, as her
full breasts heaved and he came down upon her
hard, hearing in that same instant the neigh
of horse, oblivious to the import of the scene,
about its own business of ingesting the abundant

fields of meadowgrass. And she, that other,
lifting her creamwhite Irishknit crossarmed above
her head to reveal those blackeyed nubs.

Sweet woman, Venus Amazonis, stopped once more
by the old memory of flaming sword and burning gate.

And for counterpoint: the pokerfaced one-eyed nun,
shank-straight as an oak plank, who pulled him off
the makeshift urchin's choir even as he stood there
cowering beneath that storied organ, then barred him
from joining his scrawny voice to the amassing

polyphonic harmony of Christmas midnight Mass.
O muse. Remember the vestal in antiseptic white
ordering his chastened mother from the grey and empty
room so that he ran, his frightened five-year-old
brother stumbling after like some legless beggar,

to try and stop her short of those forbidding
double doors? How the boys trembled then as his
arthritic dog would tremble when—all those years
later—he would hold and comfort it, knowing the needle
and the vet's smooth words would finally kill it.

As they did. His mother's mother wracked by her hacking
cough hour after hour in the cold dark of their compact
attic room. Listen o my God: meditation *is* like
a needle, so sweet Alphonsus counseled. First
the sharp stab and then the thread of gold, composed

of prayer, affection, resolution. Again the light
weft with the sounds of one's self breathing, stacked
ribs folding and unfolding like tin plates buckling
in the frozen waste. Eva, Ave, Mary, marah, myrrh.
The woman musing as the double master buckled

and the fire began to spread around the walls.
Sybil fronting the final ecstasy of death, finished
now with life's strange foreplay and wanting only
to come quickly. Strange consolations. And she,
behind it all, the lashed lines converging, pain visible

behind her eyes, still saying yes, yes, and proffering herself.

Replaying the Old Morality Play

Before the dull and torpid fire of his text
he stared, ear straining for some hidden
music he sensed his deeper self, repelled
by the miasmic fumes, stir towards. Long too
had that chipped cup of tepid tea stood there
beside him, settling back to sludge, flanked
on either side by crusts of sodden toast
still unconsumed, his sick head dizzy
and his eyes aswim. The single bulb hummed dully
overhead, the house seemed still.

                    And the writ went on
before him—*tractatus philosophicus*—skittering
like greenblack polywogs dropped in hydrochloric acid:
blips across his fevered brain. Just how long
he had been staring at the text (call it text
or merely pre-text), before he knew for sure
his sister stood distraught before him
by the windy kitchen door and forced him
from his revery, who was there to say? He knew
as he knew few things in surety the look
that etched itself upon his cloistral soul
when he saw her there before she floated by
his dinette chair like some blanched and wingless
Nike. Caught too the mumbled words, the nightmare
pallor in this latest homegrown comedy of errors.
And so at last he smelled the fumes his mind
had seemed to conjure up and knew they rose now

not from his pored-over complex text at this unearthly
hour but instead from the garage.
                              Nothing for it then
but once more to rescue his Andromeda, his imploding
wordless mother who had sealed herself again behind
the driver's seat of their failing '47 Pontiac.
According to the familiar family ritual she had done it:
first the shutting of the accordian coffered door,
the hooking of the rear egress, and then the engine
sputtering until the nether fumes had found out the King
his father, roused him from his haunted winter's sleep and,
domestic habit being what it is, he had understood
once more.
                    And so the heir apparent in the easy forcing
of the oft-battered door until it yielded up its lock,
the holding up of handkerchief to shield both nose
and mouth, the rapid tapping on the misted glass
where her drowsy locks had come to rest. What then *was*
the precise right tone to take in a death's head morality
played out on a winter's night in suburban Mineola?
To force? to plead? perhaps to joke, cajole? And why then
him and why his sister in their poor bit parts while
the King, in grease-stained longjohns, waited in the dimlit
hall for his Queen to make another fifth-act comeback?

So he kept rapping in an ecstasy of fear,
watching for her head to bob up quick while all
about the swirl of chalkwhite cloud kept sputtering.
At last she slowly rose as from a grave and killed
the engine, unlocked the door, then, one foot
lifting, falling, at a time, as if lurching
under water, she pushed herself into the moonblanched

sea of night and staggered all alone past droop
of clothesline and up the stoop again and back inside.
The King, upstaged thus yet again, could only stare,
disarmed and wordless, before he followed her to bed.

As for the hero princeling of this play? A quaff
of crust and tea for Perseus as a final consummation,
the text closed up, hand raised to douse the light,
then upstairs and to bed. His mind was nearly blank
but for his sister's eyes floating in the seawreck
they still called home and that bobbing head damasked
still between his eyes and elusive First Idea.
Tomorrow the text would still be there with its narcotic
hymn, its words, its humming words designed to keep
a woman's voice down under so that his noble thoughts
could march once more in onanistic splendor down the page.

The Girl Who Learned to Sing in Crow

Narcotic plash of water from the kitchen sink,
the easter blue of early morning lifting through
the open window behind the sink, those buttercups
plucked by their young and hairy stems from the border
along the rusting fence, plucked and grouped together
in her own grape jelly glass, placed just so
on the worn formica sill as in a frame. My sister's still
life, caught in this tableau gesture of doing once again
those breakfast dishes like the little mother
she used to think she was, as she sang long and softly
like the solo alto that she might have been at Mass,
like in fact a blind canary. How she sang then
with all the bright abandon of her ten and tender
years, sang then long and soft and sweetly, though
her brothers, toughened and ashamed of so much sweetness,
mocked and mimicked her in counter-song, *Caw-caw.*

No need at this great distance to rehearse the pressures
there to stun and stunt a voice. The truth is that even now
I cannot bring myself to put it down on paper. Call it
the pockmarked havoc of our growing up. Jesus, call it
whatever name you bloody please. It's all behind us anyway
and that voice is riddled through with pain. And which
of us will take the blame for the silence which says so well
how we treat our women? Who will count the costs?
As, item: how we mock them for the same courage
we ourselves have gasped after each in our locked

and airless rooms. As how we sacrifice their hopes to men
we sense are stronger than ourselves, slapping back
and rump in bawdy fellowship. So that, as sweet day
yields to day we still catch glimpses of a scrawny girl
learning how to split her tongue and caw. Hell,
we know it happens all the time. We know
just as they do it's the song birds make good eating.

Ten Thousand Plastic Turtle Bowls

And so it went: hour after
ticking hour, behind
that plastic turtle bowl
machine. That was his

machine, just as the plastic
ball machines were theirs:
the orange blond with the missing
two front teeth and junket

breasts which were turning now
to fat. And her friend the big-
armed dude with jut jaw and balding
duck's ass style hair who pulled

plastic balls all afternoon
and night bopping to the croon
emitting from his tinny black
transistor. They went at it

hot and heavy the two of them
once they punched out at eleven,
had made the system work for both
of them, right there in the back

seat of D.A.'s fifty-six fire
engine red convertible out

where the quarry touched the back
side of the plastics factory.

Even after supperbreak D.A.
bounced whistling back to Number
4 sometimes, flame pink lipstick
all over his stubbled cheeks

and forehead, blondie throwing
sidelong sides at him as she
wiggled up to Number 3. O blessed
interlude he thought until he felt

the troglodytic eye of Alley Oop
upon him, tall atop his plastics
drum, master there of all his eye
surveyed. Pork Chop Hill defender

and killer of 40 gooks (his 50
caliber machinegun kicking them
backwards on their asses as the chunks
of flesh tore off that cold December dawn).

And here *he* was with these others,
manning his own piecetime machine,
which each and every fifty-three
seconds (clink clank) delivered him

another warm translucent plastic
turtle bowl. He had to clip the tooth-
paste nibs and lay each bowl in stacks
before the next one—clone on clone

on clone—sprang forth fullformed
from those infernal bowels. It came
to 3.43 cents each, hour after hour
after dragass hour by time punch

clock. Docked time and time
again for each infraction by the deep
south couple who ran the shop: classic
southern trash and mean as hell.

He lasted thirteen weeks, dragging
home each midnight to soak his blotched
and irritated skin and work loose
the million plastic motes. But what

finally finished him was his lady
boss, shouting out at him above the clank
of one more boring bowl delivered
that he wuked, as far as she cud see,

lak a nigguh, him, a smart Eyetalian boy
(and white, or nearly so). Everybody
turned up from their machines to stare.
It was that that turned it all around

and made him a minor revolutionary.
A call for wooden shoes to slay the damn
machine! So when the organ grinder
monkey his lady boss called Babe began

to bare its needle teeth and screech
sforzando down his neck he whipped around.

If that was my kid, he had begun,
before he bit his tongue. He saw

his paycheck go flying out the window
and so resumed his shuffles and his
parm me mams. And prayed for wooden
shoes—*sabots*—again so that when

the bowls began to birth with gaping
holes in them his wizened heart
rejoiced. All night he nipped and
tucked each happy defect fast away,

hour after hour. Oop blinked
uncomprehending. It took the woman
(naturally) to spot the stillborn bowls.
Wah the god damn Porto Ricans

cud do better wuk than that . . .
an' they was good an' hungry.
So he was finished, fired, out
the door. Outside, though, the sweet

taste of early spring floating
on the night air as he shuffled home
past the dark and silent factories
on the strip, the clank of plastic

mold machines clunking dim and dimmer.
Up above, through the pink haze of light
industrial waste over Mineola: no
blinking sputnik that but a very star

awink! And thus the promise
of a million more, tarnished yes
but shining still. So it all
came down to a question

of economics. He gestured grandly
with his hands, as though to thank
the dull-spangled stars that kept
putting out each night and all for nothing.

The Hunt

Pulling the shotgun from the
sullen clerk's hand, then
sighting along the barrel, eye
level, at some imaginary target

there, where glass case and
imitation oak panel met: Click!
I caught you squeeze the trigger
in an ecstacy of release.

Ed, Eduardo, my dark Irish
friend of fifteen years. You,
Maureen, and your two small
girls, one still in the stroller,

the first time I ever met you,
there on the street of drab
modern row houses where we both
lived. Behind you: Kissena Park,

cement slabs, rusting auto hulks
and dogshit all moldering
in the tall weeds beside the base-
ball diamond. Bank clerk by day,

law school at night, subways,
buses, mixing with the living dead:

those fierce eyes in the tired
face determined to pull it off,

bust through, and screw the cost.
On Madison, tired of hearing
the other lawyer talk about his
ten-year-old track record, you told

him there and then to shove it,
challenged him to try you for the mile,
then beat him—a ten buck bet—
though for weeks after you had pains

around your chest. From crowded
basement quarters to this new demi-
mansion in St. Louis: step by step up
the corporate ladder. For years

inveighing against the cancerous
cigarette, more relaxed now, at home
with a string of kingsized *Merits,*
crossing at 40 somewhere near the top.

Reaching for the sun and spilling
gold from your fiery self with bright
abandon. As yesterday, the four of us
at the chic Hunters Room in Garden

City for some brunch, to save
your wife a dish. Caught once
again, as in the camera's eye,
click! those dark glowering

eyes of yours, my friend, still
maddened by the spangled doe
at ease there in the summer wood,
still waiting for her hunter to approach.

In the Sacred Wood

FOR HAROLD BLOOM

Always son had followed son, it seemed.
Always it had been the same, as far back
as the fathers could remember. Always

the same, short necessary ceremony:
knife flash and swish, the father's head
gone tumbling down the sacred steps.

But all of that had altered and the ancient
had returned. What troubled him was how
they'd changed the rules without so much

as asking him. Nothing for it now
but to face it like a man and wait
for her to come. So he stood in silence

in the sacred wood to wait. The rainspattered
peacock's golden bill through which once
he'd crowed now dangled from his chest.

Once tutelary males in peacock dress
had strutted up and down before him, flapping
bluegold feathers as they crowed in chorus

their solemnities. A cak cak and a cak cak.
But that was long ago. Now those bright birds
had fled the wasted wintry garden. He stood

before the ruined altar and stared into black
obsidian glass. A ruined priest stared back.
He was the last last Romantic. He could hear

her singing somewhere out there now, could hear
the swish of scythe she must be waisthigh swinging.
He knew then it was not his throat she meant to cut.

Fire in the Choir Loft

I stand to one side in the old choir loft among
these schoolchildren, listless and shifting,
fidgeting in stiff, ill-fitting dress and jacket,
while the huge complacent organ chuffs, hums, heaves
into a rousing chorus of *Open Up Your Heart,*

and stare down into the central nave of the church,
a dull gray light filtering with mute largesse over
altar, aisle, pew and column. At eye level now
these disembodied plaster cherub heads peek out
from between mock acanthus leaves, each face

exactly like the others, bland as liver. *Veni
Creator Spiritus!* Instead: a smoldering, the smell
of charred wainscotting up the ruined steps
in the mind's eye. The Czech-made stained glass
window with its unearthly Maytime blues blown

out by the violence of trapped heat, cracked and molten.
Accidie at forty for the sixth grade CCD teacher
of these choral voices blaring forth as one.
A trumpeting of victory! So the second coming
comes to this: not light nor dark, but merely gray,

unroused by organ, air or cherub music storming
heaven out of Turners Falls. Under the upturned
ecstatic gaze of the Woman, the pure elect,

sporting Pius Tenth medallions, conduct the children
safely through the perilous waves of sound.

In triptych fashion, Jerome and Ambrose, Thomas
and Augustine, to right, to left, staring upwards
in ascetic ecstasy: the learned ones in pregnant
silence about the Mother of the Word, her blue robes
swirling like cirrocumulus, as she ascends alighting

into Heaven, a locus somewhere above the choir loft itself.
From this vantage, one could peer down like an angel
on a world writ small, make notes on the devout
procession filing out, First Communion over. Even
Napoleon, they say, always remembered the joy of this

special hostwhite day, more special to him even
than his fevered victories in the smoking streets
of Paris or up against Europe's resplendent gold-domed
kings. Poor deluded lightbearer, flickering finally out
in exile, unable at the last to keep even his private

parts intact, clipped off by the attending doctor.
Call it a wave effect, the necessary seasons of the soul.
Ups and downs spinning about the grim lifeline like
flies until at last the poor beast's heart gives out.
And then the surprising transformation in extremis

into light or dark . . . or nothing. Pray
for a Pentecostal fire in this choir loft,
for just a spark, a warm current of what these
children float so easy in: for air and more air, melody
and air, a clear consuming blaze . . . and not this smoldering.

Starry Night

FOR MADELINE DEFREES

Was it just that all our ordered order
no longer served, had come to seem
a sham? Or was it something more?
The Garden Theatre up in Greenfield,
built back in the late Twenties
in a genteel outworn mode no longer
cost efficient in these plastic, post
bauhaus days. One night, waiting
for the lights to dim, I stared up
at the starry vault and twinkling
lamps of some artist's artificial cosmos.
No lines connected seriatim those
thirty some-odd dots, though
I figured there must be some order
back of all of that, if only what
would serve the lighting master.

Half the fancy leather seats
were gone, cheap plyboard where plush
had been, straw stuffing stuck
to the unattended floor, two clocks
looming from their pasteboard city
towers faced each other across
those antiphonary aisles, east, west,
both humming steadily . . . and both wrong.

One might call this Plato's Cave, call
it Theatre of the Musty Tropes, call it
one's provincial variant of the Ptolemaic
world view. Beautiful, yes, but already
dated and in need of major overhaul.

It costs to sit here musing on my homemade
universal myths, my Madeleine, and think
of such things past. A luminous blue nun,
Strega Nona astride her battered electric
broom, looping arabesques and figure eights,
all the while aiming her battering ram
against the flaking starry ceiling, jabbing,
jabbing, until at last the edifice comes
tumbling down: cobwebs, plaster, lights and all.

Call it a shamble of stars and tinkling
crystal smothering seats and aisles, the whole
dome down now, revealing the blank night
sky beyond it yawning down. Cromwell's
roundheads found no new light behind
the smashed stained glass windows
but only darkness visible. Call this
the pulsing, terrifying real, itself
the strictest kind of order, freely offered
whenever sky lets go.

After Forty Years the Son
Takes a Giant Step Forward

Whose is this face and
whose these hands oh my
mother forgive me
the long-ago as well
as the more subtle recent
hurts the wounds of the Clowned
Queen the bloodsoaked
mandyllion ver
ikon my mother let me
not at least this once
evade the truth the
issue of my own mouth
swerving already (as usual)
for its own protection
the nervous laugh
the mask your features
through the mist bleached
and mossgreen rainworn
granite oh my beloved
whose is this voice
the tongue the mother
tongue we say voice
of my voice the girl
in the shape of an
aging woman face
of my face oh

my mother only now
beginning to
understand the alpha-
bet to say it even
gagging like the cholic
infant whom you nursed

Early Autumn Song

FOR CATHY O'CONNELL

Brilliance of the first fallen leaf . . .
pinkgreen, yellow, orange flare. Renoir,
as you would have said yourself. The air
turning crisp again, flushed with the final

light of waning summer. At the truckstop
with the plastic Bavarian facade, just south
of the George Washington on 17, the sixty-
year-old bleachblond waitress cheerfully

"recommended" the house special, a goulash
which I bought and forced down in that July
heat, gagging on the warmedover mutton chunks,
once more forced back on my own quotidian tastes.

I sat there in that strange bluecollar world
alone, listening to two teamsters go on and on
about the virtues of the different outboard
river engines and drifted back to May—late April,

early May—and to your death. Thirty miles south
of here in this so-called Garden State they'd laid
you out, your thin body back from Chicago for your
final homecoming. Muffled talk on the sagging

wooden porch, the casket sealed, the long drive
across the slag heaps and oil storage tanks
of Staten Island. Down Flatbush in cortege
past black and Puerto Rican truckers to the old

Irish neighborhood and final resting place
at Holy Rood. Among the sycamores and maples
with the sound of traffic soughing past, David
stood apart, arms about your two small sons who stood

there like soldiers uncomprehending. We were here
to offer whatever last goodbyes we could. And when
the last of the last rites had been performed, he
touched your coffin gently—for which I shall

always love him—as we turned away to our impatient
cars. Five years of radium and chemotherapy finished,
the false ups and downs, the prayers like shrivelled
flowers fallen at your grave, the streetfighter's

refusal to accept the facts, the Mother Seton
pin, the hardwon patience, the yellow eyes
and wig, the meal you made in March for me,
classic French and good, though you couldn't keep

a mouthful down yourself and had to half
stumble upstairs and to bed. David playing
that piece from Mozart on the battered baby grand
as in a morning dream in the watery Chicago

light, shrouded elms arching, while your boys
donned their crisp uniforms for school.

You stood by the back door shivering, still
plotting your first garden for your new home.

Soon, you told me, we'd all be back together, here
or home back east. Six weeks later you were dead.
Cathy, it has taken all these months to take
a proper leave of you. I still see us

dining at the Pines there on the mountaintop,
the four of us. To Chicago and your cure,
we clinked our glasses. To the splendid new life
that lay before you. We sat in the brilliant air

in the still of that summer's eve, for once at least
at our blessed ease, backs to the setting sun, watching
our drinks turn to gold before us as we mused
how the four of us could have gone on like this forever.

Pastoral

**TO THE MEMORY OF FOUR MARYKNOLL WOMEN,
MARTYRS FOR HUMAN RIGHTS IN EL SALVADOR**

It was when he stopped
that he heard them once again:
the mourning doves
calling to each other.
It was when he stepped across
the springing grass
towards the old garage
and rusting chicken wire
served as lattice and,
in summer, for poor man's
Jacob's ladder, that he felt
how very clear the air
was now and, but for coo
of wood dove and the whisper,
very still.

It was the heavy branch trimmers
his right hand held made him
think again of those four exhumed
bodies sprawled across the dark
red soil and covered now with hacked
palms for the sake of decency.
And the wood dove's cry
that made him think
of the women kneeling there

beside the exhumed bodies
crying while the others
stared in disbelief
or simply turned away.

It was when he cut the dead
stems of last year's climbing
roses that he remembered something
the sisters had told him once
about the storybook paradox
of thorns and roses
it was then he listened hard
again for the whisper cry
of doves.

He needed a logic
that might blossom out of absence
and deep desire, desire so strong
it might evoke an opposite
out of air, thin air,
just as, come summer,
full-bodied roses would bloom
at last where now a blank
was scored on rusting wire.

It was then he realized
that those bodies would
unsheathe into stem and leaf
and flower, fireflowers
transforming the very earth
on which he stood transfixed.
It was a trembling then he felt

for the gentle toughness
of bud and bird and silence,
things more formidable
than any strongarm trick
of winter and ready now
to prove themselves again.

Keeping Up

What is it I wanted to say
when it should come to this:
just trying to keep up
on the erratic loop we each day
do, have done, for three years
now, trying to keep it going:
breath, beat, blush, as I
taste my body turning
slowly down to sludge,
weight falling to waist
and thigh, slower than the fall
of gravity, though no less
final?
        Foot rise, foot fall,
over and over again: a lifting,
then a falling backwards more
and more, and then the sharp spurt
trying to catch up, before
the slow sure drifting back
again into the winter shadow.

What is it I wanted
to say to you when I should
run level with you even for
a moment, as now, the air sucking
like a sump pump straining

43

somewhere in my lungs, catch-
ing your flushed profile from out
the corner of my eye, our faces fixed
straight ahead for the last long
agonizing lap back home,
before my awkward feet,
stoked only by my own frantic
power driving me forward,
falter and begin to slip
finally behind?

II   *Fathers and Sons*

It has a clear, a single, a solid form,
That of the son who bears upon his back
The father that he loves, and bears him from
The ruins of the past, out of nothing left,
Made noble by the honor he receives,
As if in a golden cloud. The son restores
The father.

Wallace Stevens, from
Recitation After Dinner

The Scavengers

FOR BARRY MOSER

Changing and unchanging they keep coming in:
the combers, washing up the seakelp, matted seastraw,
the mermaid eggs, shell shards, sandcrabs,
the seableached memories with them. Old man picking
over the stormtossed beaches, mulling seawrack
and your seawords matted in among them, I would call out
to you across the mad crash of waves, if you were not
too far down the ocean's edge to hear.

Slow to comprehend, even I begin to count the losses.
At last the image I have sought each day now for two weeks'
past reveals itself already there in sand, my own tracks
smothered by the waves a shadow's length behind me.
What is it sustains the stem of self and why even speak
of that? A self shelving on the void, the hiss of shells.

Last night the light house at Brant Point
with its steady lamentations troughed between silences
each lasting a full ten seconds. Then the cry, then
silence ebbing. From early afternoon. Even the old mill,
lopped of its canvas blades, hunched toadlike in the enshrouding
fog as I searched the sandy nub for the obliterated
Negro Cemetery behind the new wing of the island's hospital.
In less than two hundred years the seawinds had sandblasted
the lean stones, erasing all the hymnbook candied phrases,
until only, here and there, a name remained. And what

could even "Pompey" hold against that tide, a name a man
might as soon give his greyhound as his slave?
In the crabgrass soil, gray as cancer: a foot
deep indentation without a headstone, where the rotten wood
had given way. Call it the final ignominy of annihilation, loss. . . .

Today, though, new life spews up all about me: seaspawn,
algae, sandcrabs knuckling sideways, the shock of seamews
from the scolding gulls. And these ten kids scrambling
all around me, scavengers of sea-ravaged detritus in search
of treasure. One clutches a ternpecked crabshell, another
a smooth stone fragment or three lightbulbs have drifted in
from a Russian trawler. And a fourth: *le bombe,* a bobbing
aerosole from Paris with her fading face revealed: seagreen
Venus Anadyomene, de Kooning more than Botticelli. Such gifts
does the great Atlantic freely offer.

I am almost young enough to think that I shall never die.
This early afternoon, as that white disc burns off the mist, though,
I feel naked. Even my breath begins to come in shorter spurts,
my right knee stiff, these tracks still straggling
toward some vague uncompromising close. The eye pecks it pecks
its scraping way across the yellow sand, the yellow page of print.
So much to have to say goodbye to. To all these . . .
to all these. And now the insistent birdlike chatter
of the younger kids about me, clamoring
for attention. Me, me, they cry, shoving shells and bulbs
before me, before my drifting gaze, my half-vacant eyes.

What the Wind Said

FOR PAUL

Wind against cheekbone, against
noseridge, where the steel-
rimmed glasses cut the flesh.
March 16th and a smear of greasy

ice on walk and road, working
the intricate trim pattern
of imitation terrazzo tiles
loose all across this multi-

million dollar campus, cracking
under the pressure of my feet.
All week, my son, my oldest, away
from you, from your insistent, high-

strung voice (so like my own),
I have heard it blip across
my mind, like radar warning
of some unexpected storm: you,

obsidian mirror image of my
deepest self. As when you sneak up
behind me and scare me witless,
to "discourse" at fifteen

on the Chinese written character,
black holes, the New Right,
and Einstein's apologia
for the gradual extinction

of the self. Always, it would
seem, asking at the wrong time.
Call it a making contact, yes,
an acknowledgment of being bored,

and always with the refrain of
O.K., and what do I do now Dad?
As if I knew any more than you.
Four hundred airborne miles. That's

rope enough to let my words wind out.
Frailest cable. Ariadne's thread.
Trundling your Buddha-bellied flailing
body corded up in cotton blanket

like some half-inflated basketball,
the unconscious sacrifice of Isaac,
rammed wedgelike through the unrelenting
winter of my own youthful discontent.

My own Prince Hal, half rebel son,
half intent on pleasing. That cocksure,
uneasy strut of yours, as if the world
was yours. And yet you had to hide

your head before you could bring yourself
to talk of "it." Your budding sense

of sexuality. Crocus nudging through
last year's harvest of dead leaves

and fretty snow, a growing, as the saying
goes, in age and grace and wisdom.
How the spring stem holds against
the searing, ceaseless winds. How the young

grass repairs itself again. As when
they helped you to your feet and off
the field this last September, two
plays into the first quarter

of your first real game. Defensive
lineback whacking our opponents
from across the river. Murderous
and divided as poor Ajax on the windy

plains of Troy, going through the motions,
scared stiff, but out there anyway
in your bright new uniform. And now,
the season's first casualty, left hand

holding the right, your writing hand,
steady, in that instant splintered
into a swan's s-shaped neck, amazing,
as we half walked, half ran, your mother

and myself, uncomprehending witnesses
to the sacrifice enacted, as now,
your dazed eyes fixed first on it, then me,
you stuttered, *What, what do I do now, Dad?*

A Walk in Early March

FOR MARK

Of the manner in which he moves
over the yellow stubble furrows
of early March with his mongrel
dog as he has for years now. Of
the dog's limping gait, rear legs
arthritic, doing fewer elliptical
sorties this year out from his
master and back.
                         Of that straight
back, strong as a young ash tree,
of that quiet, self-assured gait,
the blond hair along the tanned arms,
of the thick blond hair of that head,
hair I have cut myself now
for fourteen years, of the reassuring
voice, the gaiety of those
gray blue eyes, his mother's.
Bone of our bone. A son. The fact
the mystery we call fatherhood. Of
the cry, the utterance as I break
the stillness with words, then return
to the depths of that stillness.
The counter-response, his head half
turning in acknowledgment. The fact
of chill air whisked suddenly across
my chest but with the promise of warmth

in it, the coarse sand and large stones
dragged up by the thick ice slabs
on the river and left there when the ice
melted under last month's early rains.
The ground with hints of green here
and there—wildcarrot—spongy, yielding
to our weight.
           Of the manner in which,
quietly, he stops and turns to his right,
peering into the swift flowing Sawmill
at something golden he invites me
to share. A smooth stone? a rusting beercan?
his dog sensing his chance bringing his head
up against his leg, nudging his hand
to be stroked. And he is.
           Of the manner too
in which, by the fact of his presence,
he has half taught his father the hard
lessons of courtesy, of keeping the voice
down, lessons other than those the father
learned for himself as a boy on the City's
East Side, how for example to rush out
between cars and huddle in the dark doorways
of tenements when the bullies had spied him,
how to pull away from the tall lonely
strangers who tried to press candy bars
and something more on him, how to leap
from tenement to dizzy tenement five stories
off the ground, the face hugging the pitch
of the roof warmed with the spring sun.

Of the lesson of learning to listen
for the faint, distinct cry

of the whippoorwill, of hearing the thin
bellicosity of the ancient donkey
who still inhabits this fallow pasture, of
catching the faint glimmer of gold
from the old stone caught in the icecold
bracing stream to be pored over,
delighted in, left miraculously intact.

The Old Men Are Dying

After the three days' watch, after the flowers
are tossed into a heap, after the last mourner,
feeling the coming on of the autumn squall, turns
and leaves, the crew comes to seal the boxes, caulking them

screwing the tops down tight, to make them seaworthy
for the last long voyage. The little boats tug
against their moorings until they pull free at last,
begin moving then towards the north, a north

more north than any the dead pilots have ever
sailed before. Two uncles gone in three short
months. How the four remaining brothers huddle closer
together now for warmth against the coming cold.

Twice my brother and myself had to make the trip
south from western Massachusetts to New York to pay
our last respects. And what was there to say? That
the old men were dying? First Victor, my father's

dead sister's husband. Short-order cook and journeyman
mechanic, his family from Milan. Bertazzo lopped
to Bert. Strokes broke him until he listed badly.
One more and I will not come back, he said, and meant it.

When that one hit him, he turned to face the wall,
turned north those last six weeks, until the dark snows

swept him up and he was gone, without a word, as he'd been
in life. Then John, the burly one, his whole life lived

on the same mean street. Mayor of Sixty-first
and First, the neighbors came to call him, as his
Little Italy turned to swinging singles' paradise
all around him. In the old photos I can see how strong

he must have been, so that I do not doubt the tales
my father told me of his brother and, for what
they're worth, I have passed on to my sons. How once
he pinned two men to a barroom table by their throats,

one with his huge left paw, one with his right. How
for years he lifted kegs of prohibition booze
and lugged ice boxes five flights down to the old Ford
van. How he once raised the back end of a Packard

while a buddy fixed a flat. It ate him slow, the cancer,
ate his stomach first, and then the rest. Leaving
his last room late, I walked down the five flights
of empty waking rooms, saw the unattended open coffins,

each with its still pilot waiting to set sail north.
And what was there to say? All sorts were there
to bid their last goodbyes: those who'd made their mark
and those who'd missed. With the greatgrandchildren

all family looks are lost. The blood gets too thinned out,
the young enter a world we never knew. Julia
and Giuseppi: left Compiano some ninety years ago.
Settled in New York with a million others like them.

Their first: run down outside their flat at sixteen
by a drunken icemen who jumped the curb and splattered hi
Siciliano, those from the north of Italy shrugged,
then turned away. For what was there to do? Once

my father sat on his sister's pineslab coffin, roped
to the flat back of the horsedrawn wagon as his family
began the long procession across the 59th Street bridge,
headed for Calvary. Too young then to understand,

he smiled into the camera. But now even he must feel
the cold. You see it when the four brothers gather
at family picnics, then turn, each one alone, to watch
the ducks drifting in the stagnant pond. They stare

at the water in the last light of Long Island summer
and, though they never talk of it, brace themselves
for the time when their little boats will be cut
loose and, dressed in their best navyblue two-piece suits,

their leathery browned hands folded stiffly
right over left with the polished black beads
between them, they begin to drift out through the once
familiar channels for the last trip north.

On the Auriga: *Lake Winnepesaukee*

Pisarro's brownblack loons off starboard.
A dozen of them diving into the black shadow
of the blue waves after pickerel and bass.
The sail, half-filled, crinkling in the rising wind.
A lift and fall so gentle the wavelets seem to touch
and sigh, kissing the hull. The world, one thinks,
is good. Even the rocks, magnified and DaVinci green
at four feet five feet, appear and disappear like dream
visions until I tear the skin off the toes of my right
foot turning, swimming with my sons behind the bobbing
dinghy. We try to tag the *Auriga* as it tacks slowly
in a counterclockwise circle. Like Vietnamese boat people,
my wife quips, for a moment threatening the bubble.

Fifty yards off bow from left to right as if in cursive:
a tern, a solitary, flapping doggedly for food. Robin's egg
sky, an easy wind, the cloud wisps staining the southern hills.
All this and a good German sour dough—old world stuff—
boursin, a provençal cheese, soft, in saffron oil mixed
with rosemary, a good Rhine wine. And our friend across
from us in his comic white rainhat, front flap up, broad
bronzed torso, the rudder tucked easy under his right arm,
recalling the night the Allied bombers droned in over Berlin
by the hundreds, precisely at ten on target under the winter
constellations crossed by searchlights. November 22nd,
1943: three five hundred pound high explosives
obliterating his father together with their ancestral home.

"A writer like yourself," he says. "A journalist.
During the so-called Great War interned for the duration
in Peking by the British. *Ragione di stato,* Machiavelli
has it. Between the wars in London working for the Berlin
papers. After his death, one of the Fuehrer's henchmen
turned my *gymnasium* class into ack-ack bombfodder.
In the last months of that insane war we took ninety-five
per cent casualties without once firing a shot back
at the highflying fortresses. We sat there if you please
like those bobbing loons. I still see that B-19, one wing
shorn, tumbling over and over above our heads until
at the last it flipped out sideways exploding in the river.
When the Russians crashed through I headed west, sleeping
in barns and under bushes until four G.I.s in a mudspattered
Jeep ordered me to stop. There was a redneck from New Orleans
wanted to shoot me there and then, boom boom. At least
they kept me from the French. *Laus Deo,* I made Canada
in '52. Ah well, enough. The air is sweet, the water,
and it is good to be alive."

               His two and our three sons
in Red Sox caps on deck watching the seaplane droning overhead
circling the lake like an osprey. Nothing more ominous than that.
Again the slap of waves, as soothing now as when
Ulysses heard their lapping. Aeneas too and Palinaurus,
on that starswept sea. And now one of my own on the bow's
edge balances like a charioteer heading into battle,
braving the upturned breeze and pounding his goosebumped
naked chest, the world still young and all before him
like a thousand islands unexplored and beckoning, as he proclaim
 brash youth being what it is: "I am a Nordic Viking, tough."

In the Boiler

When my kid brother
worked the engines
in the belly of the USS
Ranger he had his own
brand of war story to tell.

Forget the Navy F-14s
back and battered like
shotgunned gooneys after
hitting the Ho Chi Minh,
careening off the deck

and ditching in the Gulf,
the pilot sinking with
his plane. There was the kid
down in the fireroom with
my brother had his hand sliced

off below the wrist trying
to locate the high pressure
leak he heard but couldn't
see. So when my buddy Vic
invited me to see the inside

of the Number 2 water tube boiler
at Holyoke's Steam Generating
Plant downtown along the old

canal I took him up on it, put
on the navy blue coveralls

and then belly-crawled in after
him. I took down notes by flash
light about refractory brick,
about nitrates along the arteries
of tubes, the rest of it,

and peered up fifty, sixty
feet at the shadows on the
blackened concrete walls.
Twenty feet above me Vic
stood staring down the orifice

of the left lower burner
rasping off figure after
figure while the scorched
scaling where the hungry
flames had done their worst

kept dropping down in chunks
memento mori–like unseen. If
I heard a click I was to get
my ass the hell out fast. We'd
both have fifteen seconds then

to squeeze out through
a two by two foot opening
(arms first then shove)
before the flames came roaring
out. Four horizontal sheets

of flame like afterburners
on a jet. You know what I was
thinking then: this way to the showers
please, the stone faces on the
other side monitoring the movement

in the stalls, Pompey's lava
savaged bodies, Dante's tarpitched
malebolge, apocalypse by Bosch.
All unreal as hell . . . or death.
I held the light for Vic coming

down the ladder to the pit,
shadows playing games around
his face. He was grinning that
jack-o-lantern grin of his
and blinking from the dust.

Well what you think of hell now
he was saying. I don't know
why but I could have hugged
the big bastard just
for being there for me.

Crossing Cocytus

i

Arc of fire across the black of heaven: a father's fist
in downswing so that even the sun must avert its gaze. Midriff,
the muscles taut, rib on rib defined, the glint of honed mahogany.

A partial image trying to announce itself, so that one
is forced back on that and that alone as it blips across the mind.
To begin there, then, the shock at last acknowledged, and then

to let the meaning circle out, cold eccentric pulses from a probe
approaching an erratic world, the imagination refusing consolatic
wary of swerving to left or right. As with Jacob, seeing no way

out, confronting the stranger there before him, arms up
like a wrestler's, whose stance is meant to taunt and keep one's hi
off balance. Pinions creaking even yet, those pterodactyl wings

like windmill blades as they fan the long-dead air back into
motion. To circle without seeming to move, then to lunge, as now
your eye catches those taut claws circle into view, thumbs bent in

along the dirtcaked palms to keep from breaking when they strik
the muscled neck, black as that corpse once glimpsed at carnival,
organ music piped into the psychedelic coffin, what had been

a woman once, dredged up from Salt Lake's depths, hawk's claws
going for your eyes, as now you face those twin fangs and then
those glowering half-mad eyes, and you smash back at last

against him in a frenzy of release in this agony of song, horn
hard, your right fist arcing down and over, as once he showed you,
that one shot shattering (noseridge, cheekbone, eye) the glass.

ii

The horn: held in different posturings. Ramshorn, trumpet,
tuba, sax, and horn of plenty. Aloft or swerving on its a-
symmetric line of force. Horn of ibex, horn of goat. In the crotch

of the arm, like so, or lifted to the disfigured lips
to sound a way-down note, fingers on the valves, as breath strains
to hold it there as a sign of inspiration. Sounds then the self

makes in its isolation: grunt, eructation, parrot squawk,
the mindless trumpet of the rectum become a point of force.
Breath: that universal given, sustained by some unseen Lover

even here along Cocytus. A thought to irritate the arid eye.
The bugle at the Chinese soldier's lips along the frozen Yalu
so that we froze in terror, tried in vain to warm our hands enough

to pull our cranky rifles from our blankets and waited for the shadows
to appear, howling in the predawn wind across that void. The rabbi
there at Belsen: Yom Kippur '44, cupping his shaking hands

to call the lost, his thin cry interrupted by the incoming train
with its fresh arrivals. Bull's horn, thick and dripping between
those thighs, brooking no refusal. The song of Cyclops repeating

the same crude strain. The highrumped gladiator lifting high
his horn, crowing the force of his contending, throwing down
his glove to anyone who dared oppose him. And yet. And yet I too

have been given and can give. Abba: daddy. My son, eleven, playing
scales up and down his trumpet, the sweet notes rising and falling
with the breath we gave him, she and I, thus shattering the glass.

iii

For weeks haunted by a sheen of purple marble, the gossamer
curtains rustling against the night's black jade. Not that
image on the refectory wall as at Padua, Pan as cartoon presence,

goat's head with wolf's fangs, draco, demon, not that but something
else: light gathering to itself, like a dying fire in the woods,
when one starts from some troubled sleep at three. Refusing

to reveal itself more fully, yet still fixed on the mind's eye.
Jacob, with the first hint of dawn, the cold light, after struggling
through the drugged hours with that shadow, feels the wind

shift and charges the heart be kinder to itself. And sees
the light grow then less alien. As on that morning, in the first
light of the March dawn, when we walked in groups or singly,

though we were none of us alone, and the road revealed itself
ascending, we heard the yellow grosbeaks and the sparrows—
a cry, a song, a signal—and knew they ushered in the sun.

You know how the thing that strikes you odd becomes the butt
of jokes, flat and simple like some comic strip: Joe Palooka's
sidekick Knobby Walsh, shifting from black to grey to white

with the intervening years, the Katzenjammer Kids, biff boom
bamm, Batman and the Japs. False clarities. False dawns.
Those other half-formed clarities: groping for the bathroom mirror

at three a.m., to see your shadow as you grip the sink. The shadow
floating in the mirror there, though you stand stock still. The final
recognition of that shadow, those crow's eyes glaring from the glass.

iv

And one, shivering from the wintry drizzle that spattered in that
dank hole, lifted his bent head to meet my unsteady gaze. "What,
are you here, too," I asked him (though he was not), staring now

into his eyes which burned like dying embers, though his cheeks
were streaked with wet. "Hard it is to ask forgiveness, even here,"
I thought I heard him say. "I would forget the past and all

we suffered, though we take it with us into death. That day at table,
when I broke my fist against your face, there where noseridge,
cheekbone and right eye meet, and wore the sling all summer long,

it was because the words had failed me. I had a bastard anger
in my heart, had to tell you I was boss and you but one of seven
sparrow mouths all screeling for the worm. When you answered back

I felt your words cut below the waist, and so I struck out as I
had once taught you." And I: "Call it the necessary crossing. I confess
I might have parried by cringing back, but instead I took the blow,

for I am my father's son. Twenty years have come, have gone, since
that day we sat there breaking bread. I have my own sons now
and have known unreasoning anger too. That grayhaired older man,

potbellied and hard of hearing, who put his arms about me crying
when his sister died is not the other one we knew. Strange meeting,
to find you here in my private hell, where I thought to find

myself." And, as I lifted him to kiss him: "Perhaps, my son,
you have." To which I stuttered, wordless, to hold him back,
even as he faded, like panes of ice at last dissolving in the sun.

     v

What is it we keep doing to ourselves, our charred tongues
uttering the cleft gutturals? For years haunted by the boy
under the greatlimbed purple beech that fronts my home,

his scrawny arms locked about his knees, sobbing to himself.
When I call to him he does not answer, as if he could not hear.
I see him laced with the gold hush that beech leaves hold

in early spring before they tarnish down to dour purple
like the rest of us. I want to touch him, as though the years
wedged between us like a mirror might somehow melt away.

Strange how his sobbing sounds like singing. I want to comfort him
and have him comfort me, tell him it is all right now and forgive him
his having fathered me. It has come out well I would have him hear.

See: here are my arms, my legs, my eyes, my one good ear, a tongue
that sings. I have splintered into three sons myself, I have
my wife, my friends, my God. Listen: I can sing, though it sound

like crow or sparrow. Let me hold your scrawny shadow in my arms.
And let me forgive you since you could only raise a self from the little
you could know. And though you tasked me hard, it was to flail out

against inertia's darkness, that lovely death, surcease, within.
And though alive now only in my memory, forgive my not becoming all
you wanted, since I had to learn the fact of limitation and, hardest

gift of all, the simple joy of being. Thus, having uttered this,
to cease my years of wrestling with this angel, to call him good
at last and watch him, slowly breaking, embrace the chastened son.

III   *Promptings*

There is of course another stream going through
Empedocles, Heraclitus, Bruno, Hariot: the recurrent
image for the process that can see *Est* and *Non Est*
and join them, seeing the fulcrum around which
they turn, and can live—in both history and in
imagination—from that pivotal point.

Adapted from Muriel Rukeyser's
The Traces of Thomas Hariot

Following the Light

In the midst of so much rich uncertain
music he could still get it right for once:
the late late Romantic mirrored in those
giant sea creatures trussed up each day
along the bustling wharf. Eyes glazed
from staring at the naked sun too long,
"clenched beaks coughing for the surge again."

Shelley too in his own brief stay knew
the suicidal drift of swimming toward the light.
As in his lines composed at Lerici,
where fish, drawn by the lamps along
the surface, feel the swack of truth
against their skulls before they are lifted
stunned and gasping into baskets.

Crane watched the phosphorescent swale
of the turtles as they struggled toward
the sundrenched beaches. Hour after hour
he watched, then leapt at last into
the finchurned waters. And when that other
dropped over the sloop's edge, what lamp-
eyed creature was waiting there to greet him?

What is it but a maggot in the brain, the mind
ridden by that whore the Muse? Half bare-
bosomed woman, we say, half conger eel, her song

a drug, her lamp beside her swinging, coaxing
her chosen ones upward toward the light
as we listen to the sounds of words which are
not quite words drifting downward through our element.

Hang Gliding on the Upper Slopes

FOR JIM TATE

So it had come at last to this: the homemade makeshift
wings and tri-form rudders, the side- and rear-view mirrors,
lines strung out and out, the esemplastic flippers for his feet.

For more years than those two smalltime tinker brothers
had fussed to get their craft afloat he'd had to make
and then remake alone there in his sweaty shop, at times reduced

to stealing whatever he could get away with to make
his *Feathered Folly* fly. Behold him now in roserimmed
goggles, lightweight nylon cords and cruciform supports:

the streamlined manner of the minimal (though for old time's
sake he'd added all his backup safety measures, ransacking
dusty tomes back as far as Daedal and DaVinci for what they had

to say). He perched astride the vasty upper slopes, crash helmet
straps secure, extended wings dragging downward as the poly-
phonic wind began again to shift. Certes he would fly again,

as on the sparrow bluffs below those years ago he'd hung
hovering in his slender air device before he'd landed
running on his straining awkward tumbling feet.

Keep the cords tight, they were still shouting on his left.
Hurl out, then down and down in one clean, straight existential
thrust. And on the right: fall because you must. But in

that fall learn to arc, to twist, to pirouette like the others.
And in your downward glide remember this: that much depends
upon the brilliance of your swerve. So here he was, an ear

opened to either side, sporting taut lines tied to those
outlandish riders, feathers fluttering in the taunting wind.
The crowd was screaming now and waiting for the Eiffel Tower

plunge as he stepped off the tittering brink. In the high
and liquid air he could feel the ecstasy and terror before
the final fall. He was kicking with his flippers and flapping

both his arms as his mythy wings began to rise and lift
until he felt as if he were floating free, even as he began
falling fast then faster towards the unforgiving giddy earth.

An Encirclement of Horses

And now the hot press of horses' flanks
against his chest, pressing him back, the troubled
snort, staccato clop of hooves slicing at his feet.

Words, words, in order to stab at what he meant
to say, that giddy swarm of vocables, when all he felt
was dark, was pitch, was black, when what he felt again

was his head bobbing between his hands as he slouched
over the once-familiar edge. And the dark isolate form
of his wife asleep across the chasm of the bed as now

he watched the nightmares circle round at the far end
of the room for the final charge. As at Sienna, the chestnut
thoroughbreds galloping past in a fireflint sparked off

the cobbles hurling back the crowds like singed leaves
coiling. The stiffbacked trooper off Boylston astride
his charger as he heeled its eager flanks, rump haunch

rump haunch, against that sea of faces forced in upon itself.
The decentering of Picasso's horse in black and gray
chromatics, dismembered, its stark accusing eye, dagger tongue

and disembodied shriek. Stiltlegged roans half a mile
high, loping unchecked across the world, ridden by four
gaunt blind apocalyptic horsemen. Exhausted, to turn

and face his last tormentors. To see the horses down
and thrashing in the dry ravine, legs stretched out before them
like twisted rails, the sabered bellies and the entrails.

To see as in a revelation the spotted ponies standing still
in the chill wind coming off the Big Horns. To catch
the unblinking stare before the final, the obliterating charge.

Baudelaire at Gamma Level

At that depth the face disengages
from the surrounding murk, looms large
in the uncertain foreground. Sad visage.
The Roman cut of the generous nose, the thin
split of the grim lips, the long hair, collar-length

but trim, unpretentious, in the style of the times.
And the eyes dark, prominent, unrelenting,
pinpricks of preternatural light globed
in those fixed pupils. Dredged up neither
with my will nor yet against it from the depths

at Gamma, let us call it, so that now it must
be met. Had it been the highstrung saintly
English Jesuit or my provincial American faux naif,
two whom I have courted these twenty years, I should not
have been surprised when I entered at what cost I know

these depths. But this one, the splenetic
Frenchman in tailored coat and tie, black
on deeper black: I had not thought to meet him.
Subdued and civil, fresh from his private but refining
fire, he speaks with my tongue since I know no French.

We stare out the second story window of this nineteenth
century room, a place Pater or even Huysmans would have
nodded their approval at, we stare into the gray

nothing staring back. I know now that he is one
of those we call the living dead, one of those who live

beyond their deaths, and what he says he says therefore
without embellishment or waste of breath. I stand
before you to tell you what I know you do not want
to hear, he says, though I come here as a friend. Listen:
I know your mind, your heart, at least as well as you,

for I have been there already long before you. I know
too well the lines you use, know the shallow mask
of the faux naif, the trying guise of what you like
to call the new world natural man. How American,
this boring heresy of restoring innocence

by merely wishing for it. Your Poe: he understood,
knew all too well the grotesque lie of equating easy
bounty with true well-being. Knew as well the plangency
and cry of your Rachels searching for their black-eyed
children dead. No more of your Disneylands, my friend,

no more hankering after what cannot be had again.
It is no longer amusing or even quaint to witness
these twenty-year mock veerings to left to right
you call your revolutions as you stumble toward
the yawning void which will soon enough be here.

Forget the clamant voices of the media, crying *hear-me,*
hear-me, like shitflecked magpies all searching
for someone they can call themselves. That day is done.
You will need a tongue, I know, to say what you will have
to say. Meantime: avoid your fretting and leave the old bitch

fame alone. Listen rather to the promptings of what
you used to call the soul. And do not be afraid.
You understand these eyes you stare upon are not
those cauterized upon the ancient linen, but already
they have seen much that lies in store for you:

that flame which is not eros, is not ecstasy, but may
indeed help to heal a wound. You know of what I speak,
which must be for you ear alone. The very air you breathe,
saturated now with such self-pitying moan that it
must soon sink into the river of forgetfulness

from its own neckbending weight. Clear your head,
pay attention to these presences which even now
begin to throng about you. They are friends, strange
and unaccustomed friends we know, but friends for all
that, advisors, whom One has directed here to you.

Let the hyenas bark and laugh, gritting blackened
fangs and snapping at what they will not understand.
They have their appointed place as you have yours.
And yours, my brother, we will call the season
out of time. Enough. And ceased. And faded back, was gone.

A Smooth White Pebble

Pistolcrack! Thunder over my head, over
the transformed stables they call the Pebble now.
A startled silence as when the breath is too long held . . .
and then the boom rolling further north towards Sandy Neck.

The ear listens for the wind riding the stones
over the tall leeward seabeach grasses. Quaker white walls,
stonework and woodwork, slatted, strong, these gracefully
placed statues from the Gambias, the taut cylinder breasts
of the ebony totems, the painted antelope head
with its alternating crisp and undulant lines etched
against white, dart of swallows under the courtyard,
and the maple darkly rustling. A house to myself
for the next few hours, a rented place at Barnstable,
to taste like the taste of clear white wine—Orvieto—
thunder and silence and chitter of sparrows, wind
washing over beachgrass and daylillies like the gay rustle
of an unexpected skirt. And now, again, rain spattering
in gusts, brightening the pink white mottled
pansies in the cedar box outside this window:
tiptoeing off, then turning, returning.

                                        Highet speaks
of the old Roman landscapes as if he too
were sampling wine, like Simic and Matthews last year
in Genoa, the bottles and corks laid out in row after row
on the crisp white cloth before them. Catullus, above
the endlessly rolling waves beating on Sirmio

as the tortured olive trees tossed arthritic limbs
against the unceasing wind (as I myself remember),
the white sheet of lightning striking the Garda
as the wind slammed the shutters against the plaster walls.

Virgil beside the smooth-sliding Mincius above Mantua,
grave head bowed in contemplation. Horace laboring
with the others on that isolated farm of his like a small bee
sipping each sweet blossom of thyme as he shaped cell
by honied cell his poems. On the ghost-haunted road
to Gallicano: Tibullus, dark and light conspiring.
Young Ovid, kicking up the dust as he made his way towards
Sulmona high in the Abruzzi region, head filled with women,
ah the beautiful women of Rome. And Allen: deep in thought
across the centuries before the statue of that lover
in the Piazza Vente Setembre as we made our way across
the cobbled stones to dinner.
                              Juvenal, trekking the high bed
of the Garigliano, hard as the unrelenting land that bore him.
The deep cut of the Taro, which we followed all that
afternoon, looking for the stone outcrop called Compiano,
as I searched among the lengthening shadows and half-familiar
faces for the rocks and trees and light which had formed
my father's fathers.

        Landscapes color our lives, our lines.
Brushstroke by brushstroke they do line themselves
across the heart's own cortex. A few broken beeches
along a river's edge to hold a thin line against
the waste of empire, whether here or there. The shape
of a voice, a house, a road turning, a tuft of smoky cloud,
which would seem to keep for no one but slips away to rain.

And yet something stays, something gathers like a child
in the womb, cell by sweet cell, the wash of lithograph
in what we see and how we see it. As here, now, worlds
condensed for once into one cool white translucent pebble.

Smoke Rings

O most sacred muse: conspire, breathe
into my aging lungs, take fire.
Recall. Recall: genuflecting on his
right knee before the stack
of Fifties records, the whole warped
garland of discs, my doppleganging
brother chews over, mulls, meditates,
takes a deep drag on his *Lucky Strike*
arabesquing between his teeth, leans
to the right, to the turntable,
fumbling for its own omphalos,
then slips a good one on to start
the music. Cloud-wreathed, priestly
eyes aglint, he shifts his weight
buttock to buttock, half chanting,
half mocking his own ground bass
antiphonal to those disembodied
voices flooding through the twin speakers:
Bowm! Bowm! O Baby! Bowm! Bowm!
O Baby Bowm! Bowm! Call it a catch
for the new heavenly man caught up (wheezing)
in his own hypnotic trance.

As then, intoning
the Introibo, when Father Hagen, in purple
chasuble and stole, ascending the seven
steps up the imitation Gothic altar, face

forward, handed me the biretta as we
mumbled the strange polysyllables as best
we could, my brother and myself: *Ad deum
qui laetificat juventutem meum, joy
of my youth*. Rejoice, rejoice. Trace of
incense in the gray light of windy March,
a plain chant pale against the stained
glass windows, drifting out through cracks
to mingle with the early morning traffic
like ordinary water mixed with wine.

o

The old familiar hack hack cough. Flak
burst at eye level. Who was it we copped
the carton of *Luckies* from, and to what
real purpose? Remember? Remember
that balding horsetrader who lived out
in Stressman's barn (the last barn in all
of Levittown, fronting the advancing
line of myrmidons, ten thousand
identical Cape Cod structures built
for G.I.s hungry for a piece
of rich Long Island farmland)? O we watched
the poor bastard trembling jack off daily
from the moted loft above in golden light
sublime, watched him count and hide his coins
and his forbidden sticks of joy, then stole
it and watched it all go up in smoke.

As when
the priest, lighting the magnesium flare

at the Pope's crowning: *Sic transit gloria mundi.*
Why then did we steal that man's pears, then
pitch them down the cobbled streets, breast-
knocking Augustine, seeing the city through
a haze of fevered smoke, once asked. At eleven
the whole face turns snot green on as many
puffs, one learns to one's regret. And then,
to top it off, someone spied us out behind
the weedrank pigpen and told our Father.
An allegory that. *Now you have a choice, my sons,*
he said. *You kin quit this stuff right now*
until you're old enough. Or you kin wolf down
this whole pack here. Twenty sticks unfiltered?
And so I promised: no more smoking, and kept
my word. You too promised, o recreant brother,
meaning only not around our Father. Language,
you might have said, slips, slides, means
different strokes to different folks. But all
you said was: *sheet.* Thirty years have passed
since then, thirty years at three packs a day.
And every last hacking puff most obviously a joy.

°

A jug jug and a jig jig. Arms akimbo, raised
thus half above the head, limber wrists, so that
the fingers bob loose as noodles, shuffling
to his homemade syncopated rhythms, left foot
right foot. One two! Narcissus playing wordgames
with himself. As we all did then. This same tune
blaring from the '47 Pontiac up again on blocks
in our cluttered one-car garage (our Father's

car outside). Whole Saturdays spent crawling
over and under the battered bloodstained wrecks
at the junk yard in New Hyde Park in search
of parts as intensely as any archaeologist. Leakey
among the Dawn People in Eastern Africa: jaw
chip, molar, fingerbones. Gas cap, carb, unbroken
window glass, an untattered back seat on which
to lay the Perfect Woman on, the one who never
came. Music from twenty rods at Jones Beach
that late spring night. Like schools of dolphins
the rumps of our classmates rose and disappeared
in doublebacked ecstasy from the backs of Fords
and Chevies, groans emitted from behind the modest
sand dunes when, without warning, gropings
of Venus gave way to gropings of Mars: the sax
intrusion of the gang from East Moriches. Rumble
of loud mufflers, rumble of clouds and the gods
asleep. I saw as in a fisheye's drunken vision
crowds swirling like so many tiny typhoons:
a rumble here, there, some poor bastard's jaw
cracked by firelight and coming back for more,
until crack muted to soft gush and my gut
quivered for the man beheld. I pitied the poor
bastard beaten thus until pity gave way to fear
when I caught another come swaggering towards me
and the crowd swirled open and away, so that
the fearsome rival stood before me, seeking
new blood for his battered friend. His dark eyes
glowed like double traffic lights, fiery red.

                              Bright soul,
I thought I heard him say across the mist

of golden mead that fixed both tongue and eye,
come forward now and face me. I come from the line
of Zeus. My father was Deukalion, a.k.a. the Duke,
who commanded many fighters on the sands of Iwo
Jima, Okinawa. Listen, motherfucker. Here to this
desolate waste of Paumanok my chopped and channeled
Ford has brought me thus to plague you AND
your father and all of these from your Mineola,
so-called land of Happy Paradise. He bared
his yellow fangs then and all other teeth
seemed lost, at which I slipped behind another,
more drunk than I (I must confess), one
who wore a Tyrolean hat replete with two-foot
artificial feather. *If thou must strike,* I mumbled
back, *better to strike this man than me.* Which
was true of course, though even now I shudder
when I feel that uncomprehending face pucker
and dissolve when it tried to duck and met that
fist amidst that clamant sadness. He dropped
in dust, my classmate, and clawed the bloody
sand. Then that other stole his hat for trophy
and, no longer sure of footwork or even of his
feet, lumbered crashing backwards into dark.

                                    And still
the others fought, as the long drawn cry of pain
rose up and fell. The dark waves too rose up
and fell in lamentation while music from
an abandoned portable crooned on.

                    °

A falling off, diminuendo now, a drift, a
separation. That night at Beacon at the Prep,
on the fourth floor of the community dorm
(long since plowed under, gone), all lights
but the moonlight out. Holy Thursday near midnight:
April 18, 1957. All
the other pre-novices had hit their chaste sacks
when the strange urge came upon me there
to kneel facing the sacred mountain and the
magnetizing moon outside my window, remembering
the Man himself beheld, kneeling in an olive
grove while all the others slept. I could feel
the signals coming sharp and clear from some cosmic
depth beyond this room, beyond the cheeping peepers,
beyond the meadows and the highway road, beyond
the hills themselves. My brother lay or lie
(or both) in the tricky web of the Perfect Woman.
Ninety miles by crowflight to the southeast, below
the Catskills, across Long Island Sound,
his face sweated with Priapic glee.

                                        Nine months,
nine long chaste months since I'd left our home,
renounced the broad snares of the world about:
my Father's Pontiac, those round firm breasts
I wanted so to fondle beneath the bush back
of the brick schoolhouse across the street
from home. (And that, confess again, the very
night before I left for Beacon.) My brother wrote
from time to time, although he knew the mails
were checked. Things like: *Playing ball (all kinds),*

got smashed, and: *Hey boogaloo, I'm getting it on*
(A-hem, A-men) wif you know who.

                           I prayed then
all the harder for him this night, in my own fervor
contemplating deft fingers undo the buttons
of her blouse, exposing both those goodies creamy
sweet. And harder did I pray as I witnessed
exploring hands go south to moist mysteries beyond
any my fondest wayward dreams should cross,
until I trembled in my Passion while black hooded
cretins howled. And then: the brush of angel's wing
upon my arm. *Go to bed, son, it's getting late.*
Brother Clyde, on his latenight vigil. I had watched
my hour. As for what went on that night
in the springing grass of Mineola I never learned.
But with haunting summer, having made
my own stiff resolve, I was heading home.

✢

On the late Roman floor mosaic four North
African musicians play in silence, figures
scuffed by sandy time: panpipes, kettle drums,
tambourine, kazoo. The unheard bleating wah
wah wah of panurge sex.
                           As at the hop that new
spring of '58, after the evensong, after
the rumble on the empurpled beach, that moth
warm May evening when you mumbled through a mocking
bass up there on the raised bandstand with the
immortal Mineola 4. *Bowm!* you hacked between
deep heaves on your *Lucky Strike: O Baby*

Bowm! Bowm! Yea, even as Short George crooned
his false falsetto: *oh woe woe woe woe/woe,*
singing truer than he knew. And the unreal
lights, shifting from reds to pinks to blues.
The smoke too in layers confounded the earthbound
dancers as they bumped, humped, mashed and ground
in panasonic celebration, all speakers blaring
the come-hither sacred mystery of that old
sweet dance we forever tried to do.

                                 Some there were
as always stood in dark, chug-a-lugging beer
or sipping grappa mixed with Coke from bottles
wrapped in paper bags, until one, hulking there,
focused a dull eye yellow on all in his survey.
Yet even he seemed for once caught up in this
fitful music. *Rejoice! Rejoice!* I could swear
I heard him sing in his earthy gutturals.

                                   All about me,
as in a vision, a polyphonic chant drifted up
and out the high dustspattered windows to mingle
with the evening scents. And while the (nearly)
Perfect Woman drifted off through smoke, once more
(alas) eluding me, I carried the plastic glass
of beer in homage across the scuffled floor,
an offering for my brother.

                               He was still at it.
Still mouthing those monosyllables, caught up
as smoke issued from his troubled visionary lips.
I could see his eyes were shut, as if
what he was looking for could be better seen that way.
As if (again) by singing we could somehow
slow the thin incessant drift of things.

Coda: Revising History

You know it's all bullshit
the poem you wrote about me
he sd, over the golden oldie
on his tape deck, the butt
stuck between his teeth
as he shifted into overdrive.
You *think* you got me down
on paper but you don't.
It's you you got you solipsistic
bastard. And if you weren't
my dumbass brother and if
I didn't love you I'd slap
a suit so fast on you you
wouldn't know what hit you.
I might do it yet. How much
you got? I know you *think*
you got the classic tragic
stance of the *condition humaine*
but the truth was worse . . .
and better. I know, man, I
was there a long time after *you*
were gone. For two days, two days
we nursed her in her bed,
her poor head rolling
with those sick accusing eyes
until I wanted her or me to die.
And sure Pop had a temper, had

a fist, but remember, numbnuts,
this: at least he didn't skip.
Try to get it straight for once
and see it from where I stand.
Words are whores. They can do *any-*
thing, depending on whose paying.
Drop the highfalutin mannerist
evasions, the this the that.
Keep it simple, stupid. History,
myth and God. Oh yeah? And who told
you? Look, one ounce of this
Hawaiian Gold will help you fly
a lot higher than that silly Mobil
horse of yours. Try to understand:
it's dead history, dead and over.
I'm tired, we're all tired.
Who gives a shit about it anyway?
You got yr. own kids now to think
about. For chrissake give
yr. head a rest. Dig it? Here.
Here! Take a toke of this.

The Respite

So for once he sat there at his ease
in a paintchipped kitchen chair,
staring warmly at the lamp before him
flickering, the single source
of light, and listened to the voice

floating from the shadow presence
there beside him in the other paintchipped
chair. It was late evening, dark,
and it was late summer. It sounded
late, he knew, and, more, it tasted late.

He closed his eyes to better hear
the sounds behind him, beyond the rusted
screened-in window, beyond the small lawn's
ending in abrupt woods. The other's
voice kept drifting out, mixed

with the still warm pitch of mountain
pine and plangent katydid. A half-filled
kitchen glass of smoky bourbon in his right
hand and legs stretched out before him,
right resting over left, completely

at his ease. And something long ago
forbidden by his father now indulged:
the rich aroma of a good cigar, his last,

cut carefully in half to share his pleasure
with his friend. It was not the words

which mattered now, the string of word
on word, happy solipsist atop a mountain
in Vermont. So for once he did not care
about the way words did or did not
fit in place. What mattered now (that old

elusive now, whatever now that was) was
sound itself, polyphony of sound, as if
one overheard it falling from a great
celestial dark, until it filled
the small and modest sittingroom with a more

than human warmth and then spilled over
into an old chorus of pitch and pine
and katydid. Form without design, he thought,
or as close to no design as one like him
might come, with no design on him

or on his words or on that vast of dark
which was bearing down on the single flame
before him. He knew of course that like
everything this too would have
to pass, that in a few more flickers

of serpent time he would rise and drift
back in blanket dark to the milling
boisterous barn, the strobes, the booze,
the percussive frenzy of love's old
sweet songs. He knew then things

would assume another shape draped thus
in phosphor light: a spectric brilliance
so unlike the womb of night herself.
That words would once more take on
design, the leer of Pan and glint

of nymphet's frenzied eye, the shake
of breast and buttock, become intent,
intense, stiff with meaning and its
discontents. He understood, since
he had been this route before. So that

this now, this present, was a gift,
a being and a being satisfied,
an easy antiphon of quiet discourse,
of tobacco smoked in peace, the rich
peculiar pitch of silence and of katydid.